Towers and Tunnels

Written by
Etta Kaner

Illustrated by
Pat Cupples

Kids Can Press Ltd.
Toronto

Dedicated to the memory of my father, Meilech Kaner,
who always loved a challenge.

Acknowledgements

This book would not have been possible without information and suggestions from many experts. I am grateful for the considerable time and energy that each willingly gave to me. Thank you to Ron Bradfield from the Canadian Coast Guard for lighthouse explanations; Eric Brown of Applewood Heights Secondary School for solving the compressed-air problem; Pierre Desautels and Richard Kwan of Yolles Partnership Ltd. for information and for reviewing the skyscraper part of the manuscript; Brian Howe of Vibron Ltd. for his post-tensioning ideas; Joerg Lauman of Sparkle Window Cleaning Ltd. for his description of window washing; Bob Lennox of the Metro Toronto Works Department for information about water towers; Mark Liddy and Ed Dimillo of Dibco Underground Ltd. for explanations about TBMs; Dael E. Morris of the Royal Ontario Museum for information about termites; Mr. J.A. Ramsey of Hatch Associates Ltd. for his explanation of building subway tunnels; John Springfield, for damper information; Dr. Patrick Tevlin of the Ontario Science Centre for the Tower of Brahma details; the Toronto Transit Commission for a tour of the Toronto subway system; my editors, Trudee Romanek and Laurie Wark, for their support, good ideas and pleasant manner; Esperança Melo for her superb book design; Pat Cupples, whose wonderful illustrations make people want to read the book; and, as always, to my family, who cheerfully tolerates my experiments and riddles.

Kids Can Press Ltd. acknowledges with appreciation the assistance of the Canada Council and the Ontario Arts Council in the production of this book.

Canadian Cataloguing in Publication Data

Kaner, Etta
    Towers and tunnels

Includes index.
ISBN 1-55074-218-3

1. Towers - Juvenile literature.   2. Towers - Design and construction - Juvenile literature.   3. Tunnels - Juvenile literature.   4. Tunneling - Juvenile literature.   5. Tunnels - Design - Juvenile literature.   6. Structural engineering - Juvenile literature.   I. Cupples, Patricia.   II. Title.

TA634.K35 1995   j624   C94-932805-7

Kids Can Press Ltd.
29 Birch Avenue
Toronto, Ontario, Canada
M4V 1E2

Edited by Trudee Romanek
Series editor: Laurie Wark
Designed by Esperança Melo

Printed and bound
in Canada

Text stock contains
over 50% recycled paper

95 0 9 8 7 6 5 4 3 2 1

CONTENTS

INTRODUCTION

Hello. I'm Jan Lapont. I'm an engineer. My team and I design some of the tallest and deepest structures in the world. We design towers and tunnels. Look around your city. You may have seen some of our towers. Your mom or dad may work in one of the skyscrapers that we've designed. Your favourite radio station may be transmitting from one of our communication towers. We also design lighthouses, clock towers, water towers and hydro towers. Our tunnels, of course, are not as visible as our towers, but they are just as useful. Our tunnels carry subways, trains, cars, telephone and electric lines, and water pipes.

When we plan a tower or a tunnel, there are many questions we have to answer. What kind of soil or rock will support the tower or tunnel? What materials and shapes will give it strength? What will it be used for? What shape will be best for its function?

In this book you will become a member of our building team. By experimenting with different shapes and materials, you will help solve some of the problems that engineers face. You'll also get a chance to build many

different kinds of towers and tunnels.

All you need are a notepad, to keep track of your discoveries, and some household materials. Make a notepad by stapling some papers together at the top. Whenever you see this sign, you might want to use the notepad.

Are you ready for your first engineering challenge? Here it is!

Look at the shapes of these world-famous towers. What do they have in common? You're right. The bottoms or bases are broader than the rest of the tower. Why are they built this way? Try this to find out.

Ask a friend to stand with her feet together. Try to make her lose her balance by pushing on one side of her body. Now have your friend stand with her feet far apart. Push her in the same way. What do you notice?

Just as your friend could keep her balance more easily with her feet apart, towers can resist strong winds, tornadoes and earthquakes when they have broad bases.

Now that you've got your feet wet — or rather, balanced — read on for more fun with towers and tunnels.

Canadian National (CN) Tower, Toronto, Canada

Eiffel Tower, Paris, France

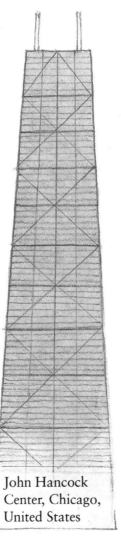

John Hancock Center, Chicago, United States

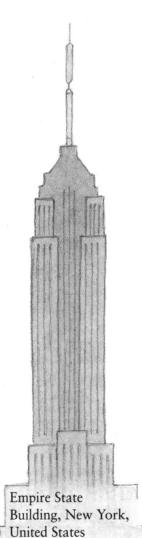

Empire State Building, New York, United States

Ostankino Tower, Moscow, Russia

1. Skyscrapers

magine yourself at the top of a 70-storey skyscraper. Look down and people on the street look like ants. Look around and you can see many more skyscrapers used for offices and apartments. Seeing so many skyscrapers, or highrises, might make you think that they are easy to build. But they're not. An engineer must solve many problems when designing such a tall building. Will it be strong enough to withstand heavy winds? What kind of foundation should support it? How will the skyscraper support the weight of people and furniture as well as its own weight?

How does an engineer find the answers to these questions? Read on to find out.

Testing the Soil

Have you ever walked along a beach and felt your feet sink into the sand? Can you imagine how much deeper a heavy skyscraper would sink if it was built on soft soil or sand? To prevent this from happening, engineers find out what kind of soil they will be building on. Before a skyscraper is built, soil experts, called geotechnical engineers, dig deep into the ground with a long corkscrew-like machine called a drilling-rig. The drilling-rig brings up samples of soil from various depths.

You can get an idea of how a drilling-rig works by trying this activity.

You'll need:
- 3 blocks of Plasticine or other modelling clay, each 1 cm ($1/2$ inch) thick and each a different colour
- a corkscrew

1. Pile the Plasticine blocks on top of one another. Each colour represents a different kind of soil.

2. Carefully screw the corkscrew down through all three layers.

 3. Gently pull the corkscrew straight up and out.

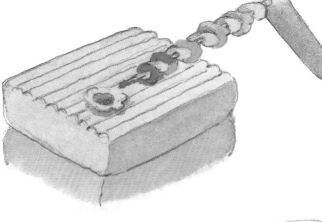

A drilling-rig brings up different types of soil just as your corkscrew brought up the three colours of Plasticine. The soil samples might include sand, clay, shale and bedrock from as far down as 30 m (100 feet). Once the engineer has this information, she designs the best kind of foundation for the conditions of the ground.

Building the Foundation

The foundation of a skyscraper is the part below ground level. A skyscraper must have a strong foundation to support its weight. The first step in building the foundation is digging a giant hole with a flat bottom. The structures that support the skyscraper will be built in this hole. Depending on the type of soil, the engineer chooses one of three possible structures to support the building.

1. If the ground is strong, large concrete blocks called footings are buried in the bottom of the hole. A large steel column shaped like a capital letter I is attached to each footing. The footings and columns support the weight of the skyscraper and stop the building from sinking into the ground. They spread out the weight of the building over a larger area the same way that snowshoes spread your weight over snow so you don't sink into it.

2. Ground that is a mixture of sand and water is very weak. Instead of footings, a giant hollow concrete box called a raft is used to support the columns. The raft floats in the wet soil.

The National Theatre in Mexico City was built on a raft foundation. But instead of floating, the building slowly sank until, after a few years, its entrance was about 3 m (10 feet) below ground level. Steps had to be built so that people could get down into the theatre. Then, mysteriously, the building slowly began to rise. The "mystery" was due to the many skyscrapers that were being built around the theatre. As their enormous weights pressed down on the soil, they squeezed out the water, which pushed or floated the theatre upwards.

3. When the ground is weak but not wet, long posts called piles are hammered into it. The piles are made of wood, concrete or steel and are driven into the ground until they reach solid soil or rock. Footings are then built on top of the piles.

8

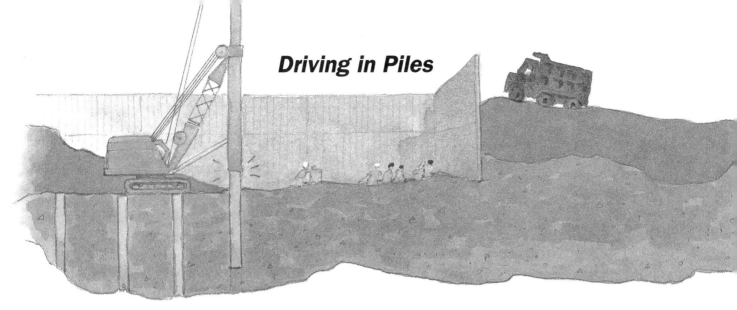

Driving in Piles

How much of a pile must be driven into the soil to support a skyscraper? A quarter of it? Half of it? Almost all of it? Try this simple experiment to find out.

You'll need:
- a pencil
- a block of Plasticine or other modelling clay, about 5 cm (2 inches) thick

1. Push the flat end of the pencil 1 cm (1/2 inch) into the Plasticine. Then pull it straight out.

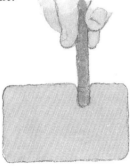

2. Push the end of the pencil 2 cm (3/4 inch) into another part of the Plasticine. Pull it straight out.

3. Push the pencil in as far as it will go. Pull it straight out. When was it hardest to push the pencil in? When was it hardest to pull it out? Why?

What's going on?
When you push the pencil in or pull it out, the friction of the Plasticine rubbing against the pencil stops the pencil from moving easily. The deeper the pencil goes, the more Plasticine there is rubbing against it. This means more friction, which makes it more difficult to push the pencil in or pull it out.

Foundation piles are driven many metres (yards) down so that as much of the pile as possible can be gripped by the solid soil around it. The friction of the soil against the pile ensures that the skyscraper will not move up or down under any conditions.

9

Building the Framework

Just like your skeleton gives your body its shape, a framework of steel, or sometimes concrete, columns and beams gives a skyscraper its shape. Columns are posts that are attached vertically (up and down) to each other to give the skyscraper its height. Beams reach horizontally (across) from one column to another to form a box-like framework with the columns. When you look at a steel column or beam from its end, each one is shaped like a capital letter I for strength. What makes this shape so strong? Make some I columns and find out.

You'll need:
- 2 sheets of construction paper, each 23 cm x 30 cm (9 inches x 12 inches)
- scissors
- a ruler
- a pencil
- glue

1. Cut two strips of paper, each 5 cm x 23 cm (2 inches x 9 inches).

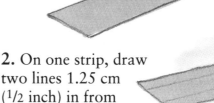

2. On one strip, draw two lines 1.25 cm ($^1/_2$ inch) in from each long edge.

3. Fold the edges of the paper up along the two drawn lines.

4. Mark and fold the other strip the same way.

5. Glue the two strips back to back to make an I column.

6. Make another column the same way.

7. Cut two strips of paper, each 2.5 cm x 23 cm (1 inch x 9 inches). Glue a strip on each outer side of one of the I columns.

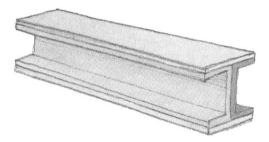

8. Stand the two columns upright. Press down on each column. Which one buckles first?

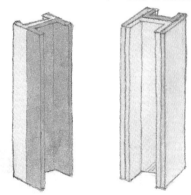

What's going on?

Are you surprised at how strong the paper columns are? The I column doesn't buckle easily because most of the paper is spread out away from its centre line. The more the material is spread out from the centre line, the stronger a column is. That is why the column was even stronger when you added the two outer strips. Steel columns used for building skyscrapers are strong because of their I shape and the strength of steel.

The beams that join the columns are also I-shaped but are deeper than columns. They look more like this. Beams are attached to columns with bolts or by welding (melting the metal connection points together).

Build Your Own Skyscraper

Why not construct your own skyscraper? Use I columns and beams like the ones you just made. Make a framework as tall and as wide as you want. Instead of digging a foundation, tape the bottom columns to a sheet of cardboard to support your skyscraper. Attach the beams to the columns with tape. Each column will be tall enough to support two storeys. Once you have built your framework, lay cardboard floors on the beams and glue paper to the frame for the outside walls.

Swaying in the Wind

If you were on the top floor of a very tall skyscraper on a windy day, you might feel a little sick. That's because the building is swaying back and forth. This swaying is called wind drift. In a building as tall as the 110-storey Sears Tower in Chicago, U.S.A., the wind drift can be as much as one metre (yard) in each direction.

To limit the amount of wind drift in a skyscraper, engineers sometimes put a giant concrete block weighing a few hundred tonnes (tons) on the roof. This block is called a tuned mass damper. Springs on two sides of the damper attach it to the walls of the roof. The damper is specially designed so that when a strong wind pushes the skyscraper in one direction, the damper slides in the opposite direction. The great weight of the block prevents the building from swaying too much. In the future, wave action in tanks called sloshing water dampers may be used to reduce wind drift.

WASHING WINDOWS

Window washing on a skyscraper can be pretty tricky. Because the wind can be very strong at such great heights, a long platform, or stage, is permanently attached to the edges of the skyscraper. Window washers stand on the stage to clean the windows. To make sure they aren't blown off, the washers are attached to the stage with belts. A motor moves the stage from one storey to the next on tracks.

My, How You've Grown!

The world's first skyscraper, the Home Insurance Building, was only ten storeys high. Built more than 100 years ago in Chicago, U.S.A., it was the first multi-storey building constructed with a steel framework. Since then, many skyscrapers built in a similar way have become world famous for their heights.

In the next few years, the record of the Sears Tower for the tallest building in the world will be challenged by new towers in Asia. When completed in 1996, the twin 450-m (1500-foot) Petronas Towers in Malaysia will surpass the Sears Tower by 7 m (23 feet). Plans are under way for an even taller tower in China, which will have a hotel starting on the 80th floor.

1. Home Insurance Building
Chicago, U.S.A. 1885
world's first skyscraper

2. Woolworth Building
New York, U.S.A. 1913
first skyscraper to exceed 50 storeys

3. Canary Wharf Tower
London, England 1990
tallest building in the United Kingdom

4. Messeturm (Fair Tower)
Frankfurt, Germany 1990
tallest building in Europe

5. First Canadian Place
Toronto, Canada 1975
built at a rate of three storeys a week

6. Empire State Building
New York, U.S.A. 1931
first skyscraper to exceed 100 storeys

7. Sears Tower
Chicago, U.S.A. 1973
tallest office building in the world

At the Core

How is a highrise like an apple? They both have a core. The core in a highrise is a large hollow column that runs through the middle of the highrise from the foundation to the top floor. Elevators, water pipes, fresh air ducts and electrical wiring are usually placed in this hollow column.

The core is the backbone of the highrise, helping to support the rest of the building. To make it strong enough to do this, engineers build the core with trusses. Trusses are geometrical shapes that are rigid — they don't move much when they are pushed. What shape is the most rigid? A square? A triangle? A rectangle? Try this experiment to find out.

You'll need:
- 7 drinking straws
- 6 pipe cleaners
- scissors

1. Cut five straws in half. Discard one half. Leave two straws whole.

2. Cut each pipe cleaner in half.

3. Using the pipe cleaners to attach the straws, make a triangle, a square and a rectangle. To do this, bend each piece of pipe cleaner in half and insert each end into a straw.

4. Lay the three shapes on a table. Push on two opposite corners of each shape. Which shapes move or change? What shape is best to use when building a strong core?

The triangular trusses in the core of a highrise are made out of steel beams. Sometimes whole buildings are built with steel trusses. Take a close look at the Eiffel Tower on page 16.

14

Elevators

How did people get to the top of buildings before Elisha Graves Otis perfected the elevator in 1857? They used the stairs. This was never a problem because buildings were no higher than five or six storeys. Once Otis's elevator became popular, buildings were on their way up.

Within a building's core, the elevator car runs up and down a vertical tunnel called a shaft. At the top of the shaft is a large pulley wheel, or sheave, that is turned by an electric motor. Several long steel ropes, or cables, are attached to the top of the car. The cables loop over the sheave and are attached at the other end to a large counterweight. When you press a button inside the elevator, the electric motor turns the sheave. As the cables move around the sheave, the counterweight moves up while the elevator car goes down, and vice versa.

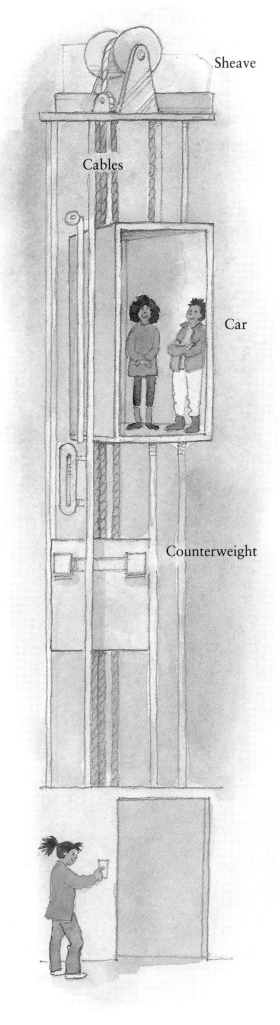

Sheave

Cables

Car

Counterweight

Q. What is the difference between an elevator and an alligator?

A. In an elevator, people go up and down. In an alligator, people just go down.

15

2. Some Other Towers

The Eiffel Tower

When Alexandre Gustave Eiffel designed his now famous tower, many people called it the "awful" tower instead of the Eiffel tower. Well-known composers, artists and writers signed a petition asking the French government not to build the tower. But the government wanted to have an unusual tower that would attract visitors to the 1889 Paris World's Fair. So, on January 26, 1887, construction began on what became the world's tallest tower at that time.

Eiffel's main challenge was to make sure that strong winds would not topple his 300-m (1000-foot) tower. He solved this problem in several ways. He built a strong foundation for each of the four "legs" that supported the tower. He also set the "legs" far enough apart (one and a quarter football fields) to support such a great height. And, strange as it may seem, he used the spaces between the steel beams of the tower to strengthen it. How is this possible? Try this experiment to find out.

You'll need:
- 2 large empty cereal boxes the same size
- scissors
- an electric fan

1. Close the lid of one box and set it aside.

2. Cut four large triangles out of the front of the second box so that an X frame is left, as shown.

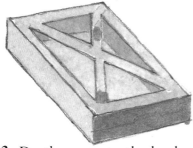

3. Do the same to the back of the box.

4. Close the lid of the box.

5. One at a time, stand each box 1 m (3 feet) away from the fan. What do you think will happen when you turn on the fan?

6. Turn on the fan and watch each box for one minute. What happens? Why?

What's going on?
The box with the open spaces allows some wind to go through the spaces rather than push against the box. That's why the box does not fall over. The box without the spaces has more surface for the wind to push against, and so it eventually falls over.

The Eiffel Tower is built out of steel triangles that let the wind blow through instead of pushing against it.

Did you know that Mr. Eiffel is also known for building many bridges, train stations, churches, department stores and the skeleton of the Statue of Liberty?

Q. What is 300 m (1000 feet) tall and is always wet?

A. The Eiffel Shower.

The CN (Canadian National) Tower

You probably know that the CN Tower, in Toronto, Canada, is the tallest self-supporting tower in the world. But do you know why it was built? Was it to

a) attract tourists to Toronto?
b) break the world record for tower heights?
c) improve the broadcasting of radio and television signals?
d) all of the above?

If you guessed (c), you are right. But as the design plans for the tower developed, the other goals also became important.

To support a tower as high as five and a half football fields, builders had to dig a hole as deep as a five-storey building for the foundation. In this hole, a thick concrete and steel foundation was built in the shape of a Y. The rest of the tower was built on top of the Y, using a huge mould called a slipform. Concrete was poured into the slipform, and as the concrete hardened, the slipform was moved upwards. It gradually was made narrower as it moved up, to give the tower its tapered shape.

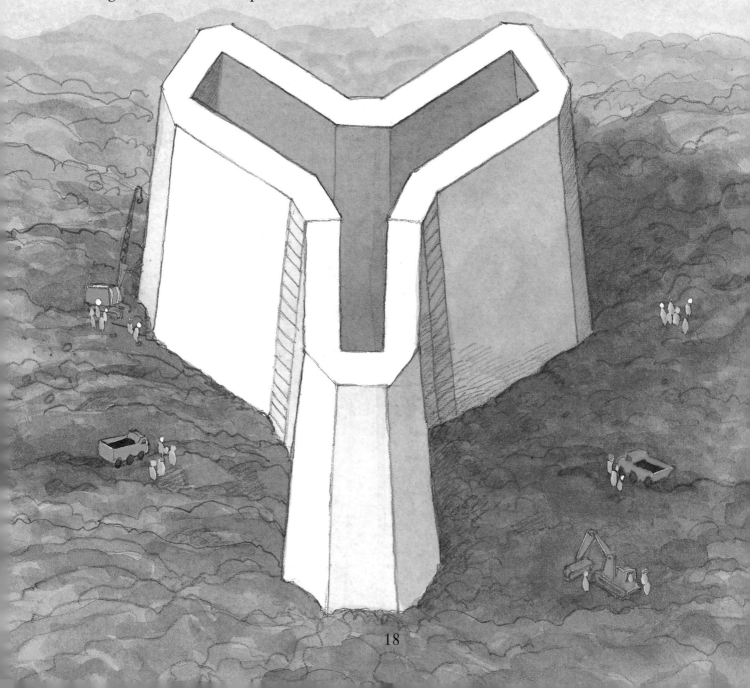

Giving the Tower Strength

To prevent the concrete from cracking under the enormous weight of the tower, the concrete was post-tensioned. This means that the concrete was poured around long steel rods. After the concrete set, each rod was pulled tight by screwing a bolt at each end of the rod. Tightening the rods compressed (pushed together) the concrete so that it could support as much weight as possible. To get an idea of how this works, try this activity.

You'll need:
• 5 bagels
• thick string
• scissors
• 2 plastic container lids

1. Thread the string through the bagel holes.

2. Cut the string so that about 15 cm (6 inches) extends beyond each end of the line of bagels.

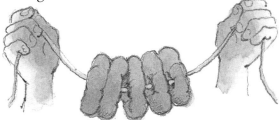

3. Hold the string loosely near each end. 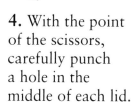 How do the bagels look?

4. With the point of the scissors, carefully punch a hole in the middle of each lid.

5. Put one lid onto the string at each end of the bagels.

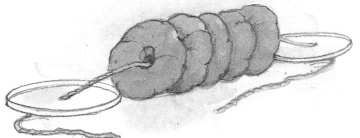

6. Make a large knot outside of one lid so that the string can't pull through the hole.

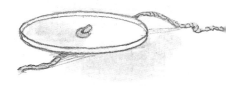

7. Stand the bagels on end with the knot at the bottom of the pile.

8. Pull the string very tight and make a large knot.

9. Hold the strings between your hands. How do the bagels look now?

What's going on?

When you first held the ends of the string, there were spaces between the bagels at the bottom of the curve. These spaces are like the cracks that would form in concrete if it was not reinforced with steel rods. In the same way that the bagels were pushed together when the string was pulled taut, concrete becomes more compressed and therefore stronger when its steel rods are tightened.

Reaching for the Top

It took exactly one year to complete the concrete part of the CN Tower. Builders then worked on the seven-storey Sky Pod, with its two observation decks, telecommunications rooms and revolving restaurant, and finally on the Space Deck, which has the world's highest observation gallery. When it was time to "top" the tower with the 102-m (335-foot) steel antenna, engineers called in "Olga." Olga was a giant helicopter that lifted each of the 39 pieces of the antenna into place as workers bolted the pieces together.

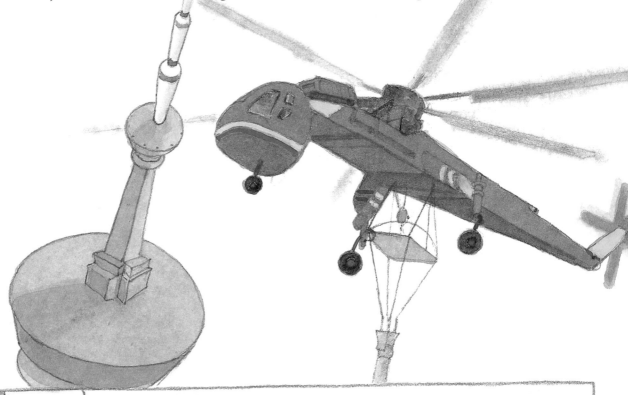

BREAKING WORLD RECORDS

Even though the CN Tower was built to transmit radio and television signals, many people have used it to break world records. In 1979, Patrick Ballie of Toronto, Canada, made it into the *Guinness Book of World Records* for dropping an egg from 341 m (1120 feet) into a specially designed net without breaking the egg. Ashrita Furman hopped up the tower's 1967 steps on a pogo stick in 57 minutes and 43 seconds. Twenty-three men and one woman broke another record by rappelling (descending by ropes) from the Space Deck down to the ground.

Troubleshooting

Getting such a tall and heavy tower to stand without falling over was not the only challenge that engineers had during the 40 months it took to build the CN Tower. Here are some of the other problems they faced. How would you have solved them?

• The many lights of the tower might confuse migrating birds that fly at night. The birds could fly into the tower and be killed.

Engineer's solution: Position the outside lights to shine onto the tower rather than out into the night sky. During spring and fall migrations, the lights that warn aircraft flash less frequently than usual.

• The CN Tower is struck by lightning about 75 times each year.

Engineer's solution: Everything in the tower that could possibly attract lightning is connected to three copper strips that conduct the lightning down the tower and deep into the ground.

• If ice formed near the top of the tower and then broke off in large chunks, people on the ground could be badly hurt.

Engineer's solution: The antenna and parts of the Sky Pod are covered with slippery fibreglass. Ice crystals can't stay on the surface long enough to form into large pieces.

• Strong winds could break the tower's windows and also cause the tower to sway so much that people inside would feel motion sickness.

Engineer's solution: The windowpanes are very thick and double-plated to withstand a lot of pressure. Two giant tuned mass dampers (see page 12) attached to the antenna stop the building from swaying more than 25 cm (10 inches) from side to side.

21

Lighthouses

You've probably seen dogs do tricks such as shaking paws or playing dead. But have you ever heard of a dog working in a lighthouse? A dog named Sailor used to warn ships approaching Wood Island off the coast of Maine, U.S.A. He rang a bell by pulling on a rope with his teeth!

Today, instead of ringing bells, lighthouses send out either radio or radar signals over the water to warn ships about dangerous rocks or land. Many lighthouses also use flashing light beams. Even though the lightbulbs are very small, the beams can reach a great distance over the water. How is this possible? Try this to find out.

You'll need:
- a candle in a candleholder
- matches
- a book
- a magnifying glass
- an adult friend

1. Put the candleholder at one end of a totally dark room and ask your friend to carefully light the candle.

2. Have your friend hold the book up against the opposite wall and try to read it.

22

3. Hold the magnifying glass immediately in front of the candle flame. Is there any change in brightness on the opposite wall?

4. Slowly move the magnifying glass away from the candle. Stop when you have made the brightest possible spot on the opposite wall. What do you see? How easily can your friend read the book now?

What's going on?

At first, the many light beams coming from the candle flame spread out all over the wall. The magnifying glass caused the beams to converge, or come together. The light was brightest when the beams converged into a single beam. When this happened, your friend probably had no trouble reading the book.

Lighthouses work in the same way. Their small lightbulbs have huge glass prisms in front of them. The prisms act like a magnifying glass to concentrate the light at a great distance from the lighthouse.

Q. What kind of house doesn't weigh much?

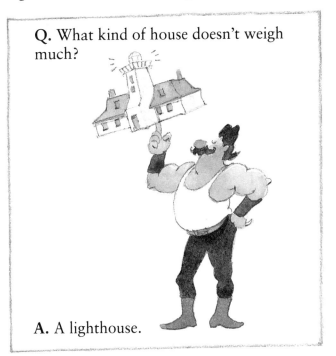

A. A lighthouse.

THE FIRST LIGHTHOUSE

If you were building a lighthouse 2300 years ago (long before the invention of the lightbulb), how would you have lit it up? The very first lighthouse — Pharos, off the coast of Alexandria, Egypt — was lit by a giant bonfire. Wood for the fire was carried by mules up a spiral pathway to the top of the 40-storey lighthouse. Behind the fire was a set of curved polished brass sheets. They acted like mirrors to reflect the light of the fire 48 km (30 miles) out to sea.

This amazing lighthouse was considered one of the Seven Wonders of the World. It was used for 17 centuries until an earthquake toppled it in 1385.

Towers around the World

The Peace Tower —
Ottawa, Canada

The Tower of London —
London, England

Some towers have become world famous for their unusual structures or events that have taken place inside them. Can you match the description of each unique tower with its picture? All of them are still standing today. (See page 47 for the answers.)

1. This tower has a sweet fragrance coming from its walls. The smell is from the musk perfume that was mixed with mortar when the tower was built 800 years ago. A muezzin (official crier) calls Muslims to prayers from the top of the tower.

2. This white marble tower has been tilting gradually to the south ever since it was built 600 years ago. The tower has sunk unevenly because its foundation was built in sand that was softer on one side. Engineers have recently buried 450 t (443 tons) of lead at the base of the tower to stop it from leaning over any farther.

3. This clock tower is famous for its 53-bell carillon recitals. You can hear them daily when you visit the Canadian Parliament Buildings. The 92-m (300-foot) tower was built to commemorate the end of World War I.

4. This tower is really a group of stone buildings that was used as a fortress, a prison and a royal residence. Many noble prisoners accused of plotting against English rulers were kept or killed in this tower. Today the tower is a museum where the royal treasures of England are stored.

5. This clock tower gets its name and fame from the giant bell that booms out the hours in its belfry (top). The bell is as tall as the room you're sitting in. Members of Parliament in London, England, named the huge bell for Sir Benjamin Hall, a very tall and stout man who was the commissioner of works.

C.

The Leaning Tower of Pisa —
Pisa, Italy

D.

Big Ben —
London, England

E.

The Koutoubiya Minaret —
Marrakesh, Morocco

THE TOWER OF BRAHMA

According to a Hindu legend, when the world was created, a brass plate was put at its centre. Sticking up from the plate were three tall diamond needles. On one of these needles was the Tower of Brahma — a tower of 64 gold discs with the largest disc on the bottom and the smallest at the top. A group of priests was given the job of moving all of the discs, one at a time, to another needle. In doing so, a larger disc was never to be put on top of a smaller one. According to legend, when this was accomplished, the world would vanish. It was supposed to take 600 billion years.

Putting Towers to Work

Water towers, hydro towers, tower cranes — without these your home would not have water or electricity, and skyscrapers would never be built. Why not try building some models of these towers? All you need are some household materials and some tower know-how, which you can find on these pages. Once you've built your towers, test them for strength. Hint: Engineers put the feet of these towers in concrete blocks to strengthen them. You can use Plasticine or other modelling clay instead.

TERMITE TOWERS

People could easily have gotten the idea for highrises from African termites. These tiny insects live in towers or mounds that can be as tall as a two-storey house. In fact, one mound was so large and hard that engineers found it easier to build a railway through it than to remove it! Worker termites build their mounds out of a paste of soil or wood mixed with saliva in their mouths.

Water Towers

Water towers are those giant oval tanks that you may see as you drive along the highway or through towns. The towers are about 40 m (130 feet) tall and can hold about 4.5 million L (1 million gallons) of water. The height of the tower creates enough pressure to send water to people's homes. The oval tanks are supported by steel cylinders — another strong shape.

Try building the legs of your water tower out of paper-towel tubes and tape. You can put papier mâché around an inflated balloon to make the tank part.

Hydro Towers

Hydro towers support the wires that carry electricity hundreds of kilometres (miles) from generator stations to your home. Towers differ in style and height. No matter how tall they are, they are built out of steel using a pattern of triangles.

Try building your hydro tower with tubes made out of single sheets of newspaper rolled up and secured with masking tape. Use the tape to join the tubes together.

Tower Cranes

Whenever a highrise is built, a tower crane is erected to carry heavy supplies from one part of the building site to another. The tower crane looks like a giant lopsided letter T. The vertical (up and down) part is made taller as the building grows. The horizontal part, called the boom, does all the work. At the shorter end are six concrete slabs that balance the crane so that it doesn't tip over. At the other end is a trolley that moves back and forth along the boom. The trolley holds the hook that carries the building materials.

Try building your tower crane out of whole or cut-up Popsicle sticks and masking tape. Remember to use triangles to give the tower and the boom strength. Use a construction set such as Meccano if you want to have a moving trolley.

3. Tunnels

Tunnels are usually built to make transportation easier. Many tunnels carry subways, trains or cars. Some tunnels carry fresh water into cities and sewage away from them. Tunnels also hold gas, telephone and electrical lines that are buried underneath streets.

Whether they are building a tunnel under city streets, through a mountain or under water, engineers are always concerned about one thing — strength. How can a tunnel be strong enough to withstand the weight of thousands of tonnes (tons) of soil, rock or water above it? The shape of a tunnel has a lot to do with its strength. Which shape is strongest — an arch, square or rectangle? Try this experiment to find out.

You'll need:
- Plasticine or other modelling clay
- 3 strips of manilla tagboard or 3-ply Bristol board, each 15 cm x 45 cm (6 inches x 18 inches)
- scissors
- some thick hardcover books

1. Make eight cubes of Plasticine, each side measuring about 2.5 cm (1 inch). These are your testing weights.

2. Cut one of the strips of tagboard so that it is only 30 cm (12 inches) long.

3. Use this strip to make an arch between two piles of books that are 15 cm (6 inches) apart. How many Plasticine cubes does the arch support?

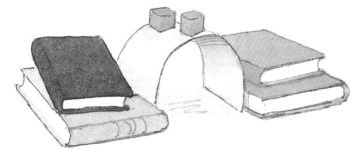

4. Cut another strip so that it is 30 cm (12 inches) long. Fold the strip to form three sides of a rectangle, like this:

5. Put the rectangle between the two piles of books. How many cubes does it support?

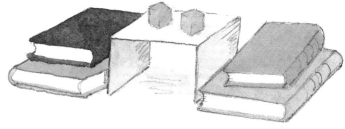

6. Use the third strip to form three sides of a square, each side measuring 15 cm (6 inches).

7. Put the square between the two piles of books. How many cubes does it support?

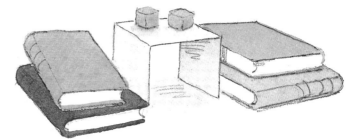

What's going on?
The arch shape is the strongest because the weight is spread out evenly, so that no single point on the arch supports a greater part of the load. That's why the tops of tunnels are always rounded.

Many tunnels are circular. Some tunnels are horseshoe shaped, like the world's longest rail tunnel, the Seikan Tunnel in Japan. Wide tunnels that are used for two or more roads are called basket-handle tunnels. Tunnels with straight sides and a flat bottom are called vertical sidewall tunnels.

29

Building a Tunnel

Before they plan a tunnel, engineers must know what they'll have to dig through. Soil experts drill deep into the ground and bring up samples of soil and rock. These samples help engineers decide how to build the tunnel.

Tunnels can be built through earth, through rock or even under water. The method used for digging each tunnel depends on where it is.

AMAZING ANCIENT TUNNELS

It is amazing that people in the ancient Near East dug very long underground tunnels using only hand tools. One of the most famous was King Hezekiah's tunnel, which carried water from a spring outside the walls of Jerusalem into the city. It was built about 2700 years ago and was about as long as the CN Tower is tall. Even though the tunnel didn't follow a straight line, diggers starting at each end met in the middle. They were so proud of this feat that they recorded it on the walls of the tunnel.

Tunnelling through Earth

If you've ever dug through earth or sand, you know how hard it is to stop the hole from caving in. Engineers have the same problem when they build a tunnel through soft earth.

The tunnel is dug with a tunnel-boring machine (TBM). This machine is shaped like a giant tin can with a huge disc or cutting head at its front. When the TBM pushes against the earth, the cutting head rotates and large teeth protruding from it dig away the earth. As the machine moves forwards, supports are put up along the sides of the tunnel to stop the earth from falling in. These supports either are concrete segments put together to make round walls or they are steel rings with wood planks between them. If steel rings are used, the tunnel is then lined with concrete.

Q. Why do tunnel workers yawn while they're working?

A. Because their job is boring.

31

Tunnelling through Rock

Some tunnels are blasted through rock using dynamite. This is how the Simplon Tunnel was built through the Alps. Workers blasted through 19.8 km (12.3 miles) of Alpine mountain to build a tunnel that started in Italy and ended in Switzerland. After each dynamite explosion, the loose rock, or muck, is removed with a mucking machine. This has a giant bucket that scoops up the muck and loads it onto a train or conveyor belt that carries it out of the tunnel.

Another way to tunnel through rock is with a tunnel-boring machine, or TBM (see page 31). This TBM has round steel cutters instead of teeth on the rotating disc. As the TBM pushes against the rock, the cutters cut into the rock and break it up. The rock falls through spaces between the cutters onto a conveyor belt inside the TBM. The rock is then transported to carts that carry it away.

To get an idea of how a TBM works, try the activity on the next page.

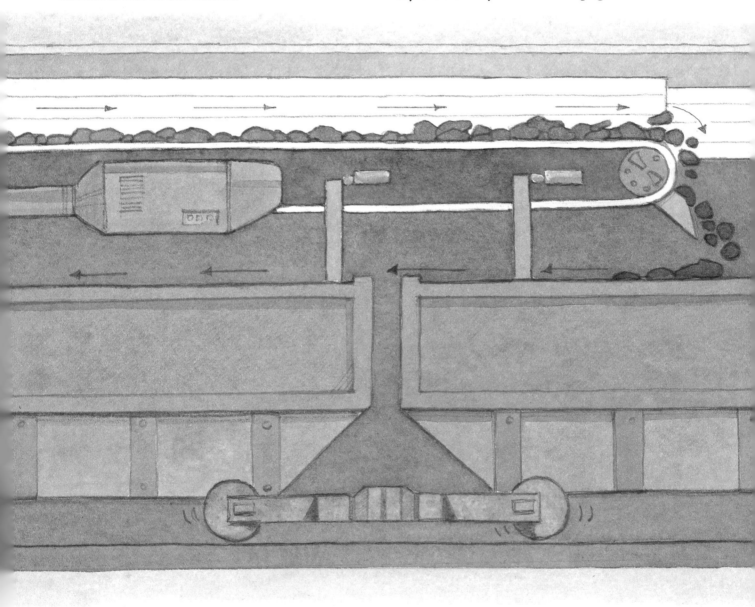

You'll need:
- an adult friend
- an X-acto knife
- a plastic margarine container
- a very thick nail
- a hand shovel

1. Ask your friend to help you cut out four rectangles from the bottom of the container so that it looks like this:

2. With the nail, punch three holes between the rectangles. Punch the holes from the inside of the container towards the outside.

3. Dig a hole in some hard earth so that the container can fit into it.

4. Place the container on its side in the hole. Push against the earth while turning the container back and forth. What happens?

TUNNEL TRIVIA

The next time you want to challenge a friend's knowledge of world-record holders, try these tunnel trivia.

1. What is the world's longest rail tunnel?

2. What kind of tunnel is the world's longest tunnel?

3. What is the world's longest underground transit system?

4. The world's longest road tunnel is 16.32 km (10.14 miles) long. Where is it?

5. What is the world's longest bridge-tunnel?

You can find the answers to three of these questions in this book. You'll find the other two in the *Guinness Book of World Records*. Check page 47 to see if the answers you found are correct.

Tunnelling under Water

Can you think of one of the problems involved in building a tunnel under water? That's right. How do builders get the water out of the tunnel?

Some underwater tunnels, like the Chesapeake Bay Bridge-Tunnel in Virginia, U.S.A., are built by first digging a deep trench on the seabed. Giant tubes are lowered into the trench and joined to form a tunnel. Water is then pumped out of the tunnel just like you suck juice out of a glass through a straw.

Cars cross the 28.4 km (17.65 miles) of Chesapeake Bay by driving over three bridges as well as through two tunnels. Together, they make up the longest bridge-tunnel in the world.

Another way to build an underwater tunnel is to use a TBM (see page 31) to dig through rock and earth underneath the riverbed. The only problem with this is that water often seeps into the earth that the TBM is digging, turning the earth to mud. Since TBMs cannot dig out mud, compressed air (air under pressure) is pumped into the tunnel to push the water back and turn the mud into earth. To get an idea of how it works, try this.

You'll need:
- a large round balloon
- scissors
- a large funnel
- one paper coffee filter
- enough soil to fill half of the funnel

1. Cut off and discard the neck of the balloon.

2. Line the funnel with the coffee filter. Trim off any excess.

3. Mix the soil with enough water to make a soup-like mixture.

4. Over a sink, pour the mixture into the funnel.

5. When the water comes out of the funnel in slow drips, stretch the balloon over the top of the funnel.

6. Pump on the balloon until no more water drips out of the funnel.

7. Remove the balloon. How does the soil look and feel?

As you pushed down on the balloon, the compressed air above the "soup" was strong enough to push the water out of the soil. This is exactly how the soil under a riverbed is made dry enough for a TBM to dig through it.

Q. What do you get when you cross an elephant with a mole?

A. Giant tunnels.

Subways

What is a tube in London, a métro in Paris, a tunnelbana in Stockholm and a subway in Toronto? You guessed it! These are all underground railway systems that transport people in large cities more quickly than cars and buses. That's why they are often called rapid transit systems.

Some of these subway tunnels are built using the cut-and-cover method. The road above the subway route is dug up one or two blocks at a time. A temporary wooden road or deck is built so that traffic can continue while work is being done on the subway below. Underneath the deck, the earth is removed to form a large trench. A mould, or formwork, for the bottom, sides and top of the tunnel is built in the trench. Concrete is poured into the formwork and once it hardens, the formwork is removed. After the tunnel is built, the trench is filled with soil and a new road is built above. When a subway must travel underneath buildings, waterways or even other subways, the tunnel is dug with a TBM (see page 31).

36

MOVIES IN THE SUBWAY?

When you ride the New York City subway, don't be surprised if you look out the window and see an animated "movie." The "movie" works like a flipbook, which animates pictures when you flip the edges of a notepad. Filmmaker Bill Brand painted a series of 228 pictures along the wall of an unused subway platform. In front of the pictures is a long wall with narrow slits in it. As a subway whizzes by, the pictures seem to move. New York subway riders say the mini-movie wakes them up in the morning!

THE FIRST SUBWAY

The first subway ever built is now the longest subway in the world. Started in 1863, the London, England, underground, or tube, has 409 km (254 miles) of route with 272 stations. The record for the fastest trip by a person around all these stations is 18 hours, 41 minutes, 41 seconds.

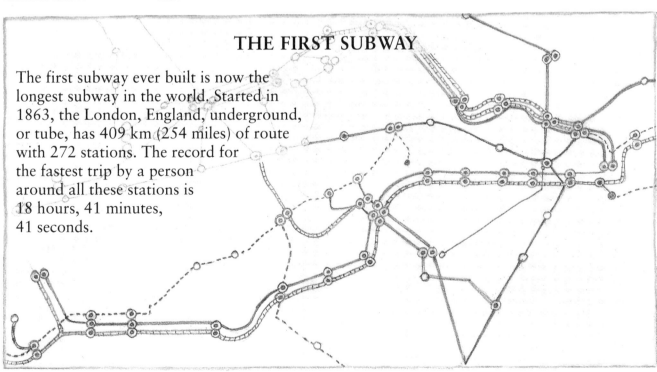

Designing a Subway Station

Engineers are not only responsible for building the tunnels that subway trains travel through. They also design subway stations so that they are safe for the riders. There are nine safety features in this cross-section of a station. Can you find them?

1. a passenger-assistance alarm strip above the seats in each train car, which you can use to notify the operator of an emergency

2. an orange flashing light at the top of train doors that warns hearing-impaired riders that the train doors are about to close

3. a wooden strip that covers the "third rail" — the electrical rail that powers the trains

4. an emergency button for stopping the escalator

5. a designated waiting area (DWA) with a telephone, a closed-circuit television camera and an intercom that you can use to contact the ticket collector if you need help

6. a yellow bumpy strip 45 cm (18 inches) wide along the edge of the platform to let visually impaired or blind people know where the edge of the platform is

7. speakers that amplify (make louder) a chime warning riders that the train doors are about to close

8. firefighting equipment inside a closet on the platform

9. security mirrors, which allow you to see what's around a corner

Making Improvements

Many improvements in subway safety are due to suggestions made by people like you. How would you solve these problems that still exist in many subway systems? Why not send your ideas to your local public transit system? They'll be glad to hear from you.

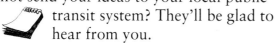

1. People in wheelchairs can't get down to the subway.

2. Visually impaired people have trouble knowing where handrails on stairs begin and end.

3. Blind people have no way of knowing at which station the subway has stopped.

4. Visually impaired people have difficulty seeing some signs.

5. Some people accidentally fall off the edge of the platform.

6. Some people can't read signs written in words.

The Eurotunnel

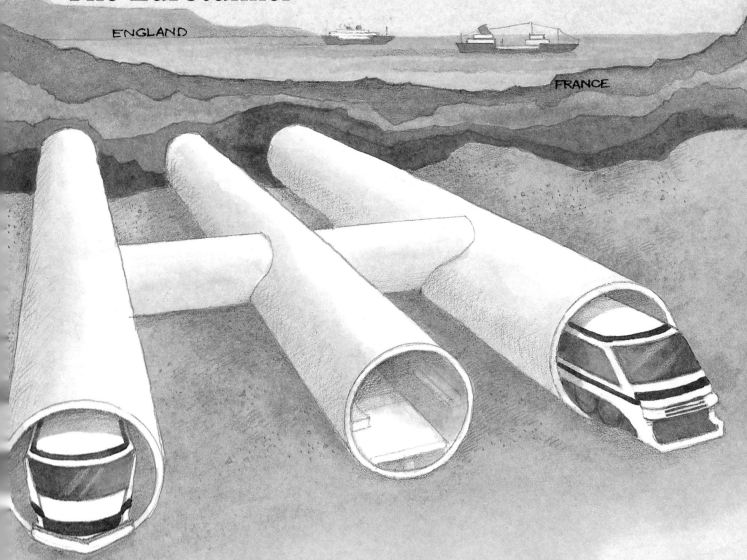

Building a tunnel under the English
Channel is not such a new idea as you
might think. In 1802, engineer Albert
Mathieu-Favier tried to convince French
emperor Napoleon Bonaparte that building
a tunnel under the Channel would help
Bonaparte invade England. But Mathieu's
tunnel was never built, and 20 more plans
by others have been abandoned since then.

Finally, in 1993, after six years of hard
work and co-operation between England
and France, the Eurotunnel was completed.

The Eurotunnel, also known as the
Chunnel, the Channel Tunnel and the
TransManche Link, is really three tunnels.
One tunnel is for trains that carry people,

cars, trucks and buses the 50 km (31 miles)
from France to England. A second tunnel
the same length is for trains travelling in the
opposite direction. Each of these tunnels is
about as wide as a two-storey house is tall.
In between is a service tunnel linked to the
main tunnels by cross-passages every 375 m
(1230 feet). The service tunnel allows fresh
air, repair workers and emergency
equipment to reach the train tunnels.

Imagine that you and your family have
been touring England. Your next stop is
France. Of course you want to take the
famous Eurotunnel under the English
Channel. So what do you do?

40

1. You buy your tickets at Cheriton, a town on the coast of England.

2. You show your passports and have your luggage checked at the customs control counter.

3. You drive your car over a long bridge and join a line-up of cars that is moving slowly onto a loading platform.

4. As you wait for your turn to enter one of the carriages of a Eurotunnel train, you look around. You notice that there are 13 double-decker and 12 single-decker carriages on your train. Ahead of you, buses and campers as well as cars are loading onto these carriages. At each end of the train you spot a locomotive.

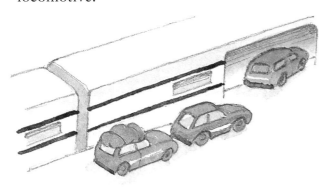

5. Your car inches forward, and at last it's your turn to drive through the wide opening in the side of a carriage. You drive into what looks like a long well-lit hall that is filled with a line of cars. The doors to the carriage slide shut and you're on your way.

6. The train zooms along a tunnel that gradually slopes downward and then levels off. But as you sit in your car, you're not sure that the train is really moving. There are no windows in the walls of the carriage to allow you to see what you are passing. Yet, 35 minutes later, you slowly drive off the train and *voilà*, you're in France!

Building from Coast to Coast

Thousands of people helped build the Eurotunnel. This is Pierre. He operated one of the tunnel-boring machines (TBMs).

Pierre: We used a TBM to cut through the rock under the seabed. At the front of the TBM is a cutting head with about 100 rollers and 200 "teeth" made out of tungsten, a very hard metal. When the machine pushes against the rock, the cutting head turns and the rollers and teeth cut away the rock. I use a computer and closed-circuit television cameras to help me guide the TBM from my control cabin.

Jan: How do you get the loose rock out of the tunnel?

Pierre: Attached to the back of the TBM is a construction train. It has a conveyor belt that carries the loosened rock, called muck, from the TBM to the end of the construction train. There, the muck is loaded onto train cars that take it out of the tunnel.

Jan: How are the walls of the tunnel made?

Pierre: As the tunnel is bored, its walls are lined with concrete and iron rings. Each ring is made of at least six segments, each weighing between 3 and 8 t (tons). The segments are bolted together and sealed with rubber to make them watertight.

Jan: Does the Eurotunnel follow a straight line through the seabed?

Pierre: No, it doesn't. To avoid layers of rock that are very weak or brittle, the path of the tunnel winds like a snake from one coast to the other.

Jan: If you were boring from your end and the British were boring from the other side of the Channel, how could you be sure that you would meet in the middle?

Pierre: As we went along, each team used laser beams as a guide, to make sure that the TBMs were following the planned line.

Jan: How deep is the Eurotunnel?

Pierre: The depth of the tunnel varies between 17 m (56 feet) and 40 m (131 feet) below the surface of the seabed.

Reducing Pressure in the Eurotunnel

Trains in the Eurotunnel travel at 160 km/h (99 miles per hour). When trains travel this quickly in a tunnel, the air that they push in front of them becomes compressed (pushed together). This air pressure against the front of the train makes it harder for the train to move forward. How do engineers prevent this build-up of pressure? Try this to find out.

You'll need:
• 2 empty paper-towel tubes
• scissors
• a cotton ball

1. Cut four holes evenly spaced along one side of one tube. Make each hole about the same size.

2. Put the cotton ball at one end of the tube without the holes.

3. Hold the end of the tube with the cotton ball about 5 cm (2 inches) from your mouth. Take a deep breath and blow into the tube. Note where the ball lands.

4. Do the same thing with the other tube. Make sure you use the same amount of breath. Where does the ball land this time?

What happens if you change the size of the holes? you change the number of holes?

What's going on?

The cotton ball travelled through the tube and beyond when the pressure of your breath pushed it. When you blew into the tube with the holes, some of that pressure escaped through the holes. That's why the cotton ball did not go as far as it did from the tube with no holes.

All along the Eurotunnel, there are piston-relief tunnels that connect the two main tunnels. Like the holes in the cardboard tube, the holes connecting the main tunnels to the piston-relief tunnels allow built-up air pressure to escape.

CHAMPION TUNNELLERS

If animals held a tunnel-digging contest, moles would win hands, er ... paws down. In fact, they could easily compete with the TBMs used for digging the Eurotunnel. Moles have such powerful front limbs that they can dig a tunnel 100 m (328 feet) long in less than a day.

Why do they dig so many tunnels? Moles spend most of their life underground. As well as eating, sleeping, raising young and storing food, they go on mole patrol. They look for meals of earthworms, insects and snails that have dropped into the tunnel from its walls.

Glossary

beam: a horizontal length of concrete or steel that joins with columns to form the framework of a building

boom: the horizontal part of a tower crane

column: a vertical length of concrete or steel that supports the weight of a building. Columns join with beams to form a building's framework

core: a large area that runs up through the middle of a highrise and holds equipment such as elevators, pipes and wiring

drilling-rig: a corkscrew-like machine that brings up soil samples from different depths

footing: a large concrete block placed at the bottom of a foundation to support a column of a building

formwork: a wooden mould into which fresh concrete is placed

foundation: the part of a building that is below ground level

framework: a structure of columns, walls and beams that join, usually at right angles, to give a building its shape

mucking machine: a machine that is used to scoop up loose rock and load it onto a conveyor belt when a tunnel is being dug

pile: a long post that is sometimes driven deep into the ground to support a footing of a foundation

piston-relief tunnel: a smaller tunnel that connects to a main tunnel to allow air pressure to escape

post-tensioned concrete: concrete that is strengthened by tightening steel rods or wires that run through the concrete

raft: a giant concrete block that is sometimes used to support the foundation. It allows the building to "float" on the supporting soil.

slipform: a moveable mould used to give fresh concrete a special shape

truss: a structure using a series of connected triangular shapes to strengthen part of a building

tuned mass damper: a heavy concrete block at the top of some skyscrapers used to reduce the amount of swaying from wind

tunnel-boring machine (TBM): a machine with a rotating disc at its head used for digging a tunnel

wind drift: the horizontal distance that a skyscraper sways from its stationary position

Answers

Towers around the World, p. 24
1-E, 2-C, 3-A, 4-B, 5-D

Tunnel Trivia, p. 33
1. the Seikan rail tunnel, 53.85km
(33.46 miles) long

2. New York West Delaware water supply
tunnel, 169 km (105 miles) long

3. the London Underground, 408 km
(254 miles) long

4. St. Gotthard road tunnel, 16.32 km
(10.14 miles) long

5. Chesapeake Bay bridge-tunnel, 28.4 km
(17.65 miles) long

Index